# A Prayer Book for Catholic Families

A Prayer Book for Catholic Families

Loyola Press

Chicago

Loyola Press

3441 North Ashland Avenue
Chicago, Illinois 60657
1-800-621-1008

Cover and interior art: Inguna Irbe; interior design: Amy Olson

Some of the prayers and commentary originally appeared in *A Prayer Primer
for Catholic Families,* © 1997 Loyola Press.

Copyright acknowledgments appear on page 205 and constitute a continu-
ation of this copyright page.

**Library of Congress Cataloging-in-Publication Data**

A prayer book for Catholic families / [edited by Christopher Anderson,
    Susan Gleason Anderson, and LaVonne Neff].
        p.    cm.
    Includes bibliographical references and index.
    ISBN 0-8294-1076-7
    1. Catholic Church—Prayer-books and devotions—English.
2. Family—Prayer-books and devotions—English.  I. Anderson,
Christopher.  II. Anderson, Susan Gleason.  III. Neff, LaVonne.
BX2170.F3P73    1998
242'.802—dc21                                                    97-49896
                                                                    CIP


98 99 00 01 02 / 10 9 8 7 6 5 4 3 2 1

# Contents

# A Heritage of Family Prayer

chapter one

For most of us, our introduction to faith came from family members. Our fathers and mothers, brothers and sisters, grandparents, aunts, and uncles helped shape our physical, emotional, intellectual, and social development. They also played a major role in our spiritual formation. And now that we are adults, we in turn are influencing the spiritual lives of our younger siblings, our nieces and nephews, and—especially—our children.

The Catholic church recognizes and affirms this primary place of the family in religious formation. Documents of the Second Vatican Council called the family "the domestic church." In the family, new Christians are born, and young people have their first experiences of God.

If faith begins in the family, so does prayer. Prayer expresses the faith we already have. It helps our faith to grow and mature. As we relate with our family members day by day, we can be learning how to relate with God through prayer.

# Many Ways to Pray

Prayer can be described in various ways:

Prayer is the lifting of the mind, heart, and will to God.

Prayer is conversation with God, both speaking and listening.

Prayer is a gift that enables us to be in relationship with the One who is our Creator, Redeemer, and God.

Prayer helps to form our faith. An ancient maxim of the church teaches us: *As we pray, so we believe.* And our daily experience shows us that we believe, so we act. Thus prayer turns us into the people we pray to become.

Vocal prayer—prayer that is spoken aloud— is only one of many forms of prayer. Some prayers are spoken silently, in the heart. Some prayers use no words at all. When we pray aloud, we may express our concerns in our own words. We may praise God in song or poetry. Or we may use prayer formulas like the ones in this book.

# Prayer Models

Prayer, of course, is much more than the formulas we learned as children. But formulas—prayer models—are an excellent way to learn to pray. When Jesus' disciples came to him and said, "Lord, teach us to pray," he gave them the words of the Lord's Prayer. Throughout Christian history, this prayer has been the classic model for Christian prayer.

Prayer models give us time-honored words that have helped to shape the Christian community. As we repeat the words, we join Christians from all ages and all places. We come to God with Middle Eastern fishermen of two thousand years ago, the fourth-century African bishop St. Augustine, the fifteenth-century warrior St. Joan, Mother Teresa of Calcutta, and our own great-grandparents, besides the people with whom we live, work, study, play, and go to church.

Prayer models express the community's identity and the way we worship God together. Favorite prayer models likewise express a family's identity and help to create an atmosphere of faith.

# A Book You Can Use

*A Prayer Book for Catholic Families* is a book of prayer models that are the heritage of every Catholic—prayers for holy days and ordinary days; prayers of blessing and contrition, sorrow and rejoicing, petition and thanksgiving. It is a book to dip into when you want a prayer for a special occasion, a book to refer to when your memory needs jogging about a familiar prayer, a book to use daily if you want to gather your family for morning or evening prayers. It is not an encyclopedic collection of every prayer known to the church, but rather a practical book you can keep close at hand.

This book was designed for hard use. It is small, so little hands and hands that have lost their strength can hold it. The prayers are printed in a comfortable size, so young readers and grandparents can easily read them. The Contents page at the front of the book and the list of prayers at the end can help you quickly find the right prayer for every need.

This is not just a pretty book to look at and put on a shelf. It is a tool to help your family—parents and children, grandparents and guests—pray together.

# A Time and a Place

Creating a family prayer life is an important responsibility. It means making time and space for prayer—admittedly, not easy to do in today's busy society with so many competing activities. Yet this busy-ness may make it even more important for families to find time to pray together.

Mealtime graces and bedtime blessings are remembered long after children grow up, leave home, and have children of their own. Many families also make time for more extended prayers, perhaps just before or just after the evening meal while the family is still at table.

Choose a time and place for your family to pray together, and keep this book nearby—on the dinner table or a nightstand, or within reach of your most comfortable sofa. Then, when prayer time comes, you'll be ready.

# Praying with Children

Even the youngest children can be part of family prayer. They can learn to hold hands and to be quietly attentive during grace and bedtime prayers. The first prayer children should learn is only one word long—they can say "amen" after prayers led by others.

As children grow, they can take a greater role in family prayer life. Build their interest by giving them parts to say and tasks to perform, such as bringing the prayer book or lighting a candle.

As they begin school, they should begin learning common prayers of the Catholic tradition. Teach them the sign of the cross, the Lord's Prayer, and the Hail Mary, as well as the responses said at Mass. Don't wait for them to learn these prayers at church or as a school assignment. Introduce them in the context of your own family prayer times.

Older children can choose prayers, lead prayers, or make up prayers of their own. They may want to sing, meditate, listen to a recording, or discuss their intentions. Variety in prayer will help keep children interested and, at the same time, broaden their faith experience.

While it is natural for junior-high and high-school-aged children to not always want to be part of the family prayer, it is important to continue to invite them. They should feel welcome not only by your words but also by the beauty and power of the experience. At times adults should let children have their space. Even when the children choose not to participate, they will draw strength from their experience of the family as a praying community.

# A Lifelong Blessing

Praying families make lasting impressions on all their members. Though children grow up and leave home, they never forget the faith environment of their earliest years. We hope that this collection of prayers will help you and your family to discover the rich heritage of Catholic prayer and, as you pray together, to recognize God's presence within your family life. We pray that for you and your family, prayer will become a lifelong resource and blessing.

# Favorite Prayers

chapter two

# Here are prayers for those

just learning to pray—the very young, those new to faith—as well as for those whose entire life has been bathed in prayer. These familiar prayers are the heritage of all Catholic Christians, ancient as the faith itself and new as the faith we bring to each new day.

# Amen

The word "amen" means "truly" or "certainly" or, simply, "yes." Ancient Hebrews and Greek-speaking Christians ended their prayers with this hearty affirmation, just as we do today. When we say "amen" at the end of a prayer, we add our agreement to everything in the prayer. "Amen" can be the first prayer of a small child, the last prayer of a dying person, and the only prayer of a person whose body, mind, or soul is weak. It is a prayer of the heart.

*Amen!*

# The Sign of the Cross

The most basic prayer in the Catholic Christian tradition is the sign of the cross. We often begin our prayers and our liturgy by tracing the shape of the cross on our bodies while speaking the names of the Trinity. Whenever we make the sign of the cross, we recall our baptism, because it was at our baptism that we were first marked with the sign of the cross and claimed for Christ. The words of this prayer confess our faith in God as Trinity, and thus the prayer is a kind of creed. It is also used frequently as a blessing ritual, and it is common to speak of making the sign of the cross as "blessing oneself."

*In the name of the Father, and of the Son, and of the Holy Spirit.*

*Amen.*

# The Doxology

In these few lines, we express our faith in God's Trinity (that the one and only God exists in three Persons) and eternity (that God has no beginning or end). The Doxology, a Greek word meaning "words of praise," is often used in prayer services and devotions, especially in the Rosary and in Morning and Evening Prayer.

*Glory to the Father,*
*and to the Son,*
*and to the Holy Spirit:*
*as it was in the beginning,*
*is now,*
*and will be for ever. Amen.*

# The Lord's Prayer

The Lord's Prayer, or the Our Father, is the prayer Jesus gave his disciples when they asked him to teach them to pray (see Luke 11:1–4 and Matthew 6:9–15), and for twenty centuries Christians have used this prayer as a model. Families often pray the Our Father with hands joined or raised up to God.

Over seven hundred years ago, St. Thomas Aquinas wrote: "The Lord's Prayer is the most perfect of prayers. . . . In it we ask, not only for all the things we can rightly desire, but also in the sequence that they should be desired. This prayer not only teaches us to ask for things, but also in what order we should desire them."[1] Look at the sequence of requests and praises, line by line. What does the Lord's Prayer teach us about how to pray?

*Our Father, who art in heaven,*
*hallowed be thy name;*
*thy kingdom come;*
*thy will be done on earth as it is in heaven.*
*Give us this day our daily bread;*
*and forgive us our trespasses*
*as we forgive those who trespass against us;*

*and lead us not into temptation,*

*but deliver us from evil.*

Frequently added to the Lord's Prayer is the following doxology (words of praise). It is not in the scriptural texts, but Christians have prayed it from the earliest days of the church. We recite it when we pray the Lord's Prayer during Mass.

*For the kingdom, the power and the glory are yours,*

*now and for ever.*

*Amen.*

# The Apostles' Creed

No one knows when or where this creed was first used, though it was probably several centuries after the apostles' time. Whatever its historical origins, it expresses the most important truths about the nature of God that Catholics hold. When we say the Apostles' Creed, we affirm our belief in God as Trinity: Father, Son, and Holy Spirit. The Apostles' Creed is used in personal prayer, devotions, and some liturgical settings. It is most widely said during the Rosary and at children's Masses.

*I believe in God, the Father almighty,*
*creator of heaven and earth.*

*I believe in Jesus Christ, his only Son, our Lord.*
*He was conceived by the power of*

*the Holy Spirit*

*and born of the Virgin Mary.*

*He suffered under Pontius Pilate,*

*was crucified, died, and was buried.*

*He descended to the dead.*

*On the third day he rose again.*

*He ascended into heaven,*

*and is seated at the right hand of the Father.*

*He will come again to judge the living*

*and the dead.*

*I believe in the Holy Spirit,*

*the holy catholic Church,*

*the communion of saints,*

*the forgiveness of sins,*

*the resurrection of the body,*

*and the life everlasting. Amen.*

# A Prayer to the Holy Spirit

When we pray, we usually address God the Father or God the Son (Jesus). But because each person of the Trinity is equally God, it is also possible to address our prayer to the Holy Spirit, as does this ancient prayer.

LEADER:

*Come, Holy Spirit, fill the hearts of your faithful.*

ALL:

*And kindle in them the fire of your love.*

LEADER:

*Send forth your Spirit and they shall be created.*

ALL:

*And you will renew the face of the earth.*

LEADER:

*Let us pray.*

*Lord,*
*by the light of the Holy Spirit*
*you have taught the hearts of your faithful.*
*In the same Spirit*
*help us to relish what is right*
*and always rejoice in your consolation.*
*We ask this through Christ our Lord.*

ALL:

*Amen.*[2]

# Anima Christi

This prayer comes from the early fourteenth century. It was used during private devotion to the Eucharist. The author is unknown, but St. Ignatius of Loyola knew the prayer and recommended it in his *Spiritual Exercises*. The title of the prayer is Latin for "Soul of Christ."

*Soul of Christ, sanctify me.*
*Body of Christ, heal me.*
*Blood of Christ, fill me.*
*Water from the side of Christ, wash me.*
*Passion of Christ, strengthen me.*
*Good Jesus, hear me.*
*In your wounds, shelter me.*
*From turning away, keep me.*

*From the evil one, protect me.*

*At the hour of my death, call me.*

*Into your presence, lead me,*

*to praise you with all your saints*

*for ever and ever.*

*Amen.*[3]

# Theological Virtues

In Catholic teaching, three virtues are identified as gifts from God: faith, hope, and love. These are called the theological virtues, and they are listed together in Paul's First Letter to the Corinthians (13:13). All other human virtues are rooted in these three. The following prayers focus on each of the theological virtues.

## An Act of Faith

*O God, I firmly believe all the truths*
*   that you have revealed*
*and that you teach us through your church,*
*for you are truth itself*
*and can neither deceive nor be deceived.*

## An Act of Hope

*O God, I hope with complete trust that you will*

*give me,*

*through the merits of Jesus Christ,*

*all necessary grace in this world*

*and everlasting life in the world to come,*

*for this is what you have promised*

*and you always keep your promises.*

## An Act of Love

*O God, I love you above all things,*

*with whole heart and soul,*

*because you are all good and worthy of all my love;*

*I love my neighbor as I love myself for the love of you.*

*I forgive all who have injured me,*

*and I ask pardon of all whom I have injured.*

# A Prayer for Vocations

Although the word "vocation" is most frequently associated with religious vocations to the priesthood or to religious life, every state of life is really a vocation, or a calling. Thus the married life, the single life, and the religious life are all Christian vocations. It is part of Catholic tradition to pray for God's guidance to help us find the way of life to which God is calling us.

*Lord, let me know clearly*
*the work which you are calling me to do in life.*
*And grant me every grace I need to answer your call*
*with courage and love and lasting dedication*
*    to your will.*

*Amen.*

# Prayer to a Guardian Angel

According to popular Catholic belief, each person has a special angel who watches over him or her. Though this widespread belief has never been a part of official church teachings, guardian angels are honored on October 2. Here is the traditional prayer:

*Angel of God, my guardian dear,*
*To whom God's love entrusts me here,*
*Ever this day be at my side,*
*To light and guard, to rule and guide.*

And here is the prayer in contemporary language:

*Angel sent by God to guide me,*
*be my light and walk beside me;*
*be my guardian and protect me;*
*on the paths of life direct me.*

# Blessings and Graces

chapter three

Catholics love blessings. Our most basic blessing is the sign of the cross, with which we bless ourselves and our loved ones. But there are many and more elaborate means by which we invite God's favor. Prayers of blessing appear throughout scripture. There is also an entire book of liturgical blessings offered by the church for various people and occasions. In addition, prayers of blessing are used to consecrate objects and spaces for sacred use.

We may ask priests to bless us, but the act of blessing is not reserved to the priesthood. In the baptismal rite, parents and godparents are invited to mark the child to be baptized with the sign of the cross. This can be the first of many opportunities for parents to invite God's favor on their children. Some parents bless their children regularly—at bedtime, at mealtimes, or whenever children leave the house.

Blessing of and giving thanks for food is an important aspect of all religious traditions. Christians find the tradition in both the Old and New Testaments. When we bless our food, we stop and remember that all good things come from God. We ask God's blessing on the food and all those who are gathered to share it.

The act of blessing sometimes makes use of sacramentals, such as holy water. Sometimes the ritual includes only prayer and gesture. Here are some prayers of blessing to serve as models for your family blessing rituals.

# Moses' Blessing of the Israelites

*The Lord bless you and keep you;*

*the Lord make his face to shine upon you, and be*

*gracious to you;*

*the Lord lift up his countenance upon you, and give*

*you peace.*

NUMBERS 6:24–26

# Jacob's Blessing of Isaac

*May God give you of the dew of heaven,*

*and of the fatness of the earth,*

*and plenty of grain and wine.*

GENESIS 27:28

# A Blessing of Children

The parents say:

*Father,*

*inexhaustible source of life and author of all good,*

*we bless you and we thank you*

*for brightening our communion of love by your*
*    gift of children.*

*Grant that our children [child] will find in the life*

*of this family such inspiration*

*that they [he/she] will strive always for what is*
*    right and good*

*and one day, by your grace,*

*reach their [his/her] home in heaven.*

*We ask this through Christ our Lord.*

*Amen.*

The children respond, while making the sign of the cross:

*May the Lord Jesus, who loved children,*
*bless us and keep us in his love,*
*now and for ever.*

*Amen.*[4]

# A Shorter Blessing of Children

*May the Lord keep you*
*and make you grow in his love,*
*so that you may live worthy of the calling*
    *he has given you,*
*now and for ever.*

*Amen.*[5]

We offer you
grateful praise
for the gift
of life.

# A Birthday Blessing for an Adult

*God of all creation,*

*we offer you grateful praise for the gift of life.*

*Hear the prayers of [Name], your servant,*

*who recalls today the day of his [her] birth*

*and rejoices in your gifts of life and love, family*
*    and friends.*

*Bless him [her] with your presence*

*and surround him [her] with your love*

*that he [she] may enjoy many happy years,*

*all of them pleasing to you.*

*We ask this through Christ our Lord.*

*Amen.*

# A Birthday Blessing for a Child

*Loving God,*

*you created all the people of the world,*

*and you know each of us by name.*

*We thank you for [Name], who today celebrates*

*his [her] birthday.*

*Bless him [her] with your love and friendship*

*that he [she] may grow in wisdom, knowledge,*

*and grace.*

*May he [she] love his [her] family always*

*and be faithful to his [her] friends.*

*Grant this through Christ our Lord.*

*Amen.*[6]

# A Blessing for a Sick Child

*Father of mercy and God of all consolation,*

*you show tender care for all your creatures*

*and give health of soul and body.*

*Raise up this child from his [her] sickness.*

*Then, growing in wisdom and grace in your*

*sight and ours,*

*he [she] will serve you all the days of his [her] life*

*in uprightness and holiness*

*and offer the thanksgiving due to your mercy.*

*We ask this through Christ our Lord.*

*Amen.*[7]

# Grace before Meals

The leader makes the sign of the cross and says these words:

*Bless us, O Lord, and these your gifts*
*which we are about to receive from your goodness.*
*Through Christ our Lord.*

*Amen.*

Or the leader says:

*In peace let us pray to the Lord.*

*Let each of us be mindful*
*of all that we have received from his hands*
*and for which we give thanks:*
*food, family, friends,*
*work, health, and happy memories.*

(Pause for silent prayer.)

*In giving thanks we are blessed.*

*Amen.*

# Grace after Meals

*We give you thanks for all your gifts, almighty God,*
*living and reigning now and for ever.*

*Amen.*

# A Prayer of Thanksgiving

This psalm of praise makes a lovely table grace either before or after meals.

*May God be gracious to us and bless us*

*and make his face to shine upon us.*

*The earth has yielded its increase;*

*God, our God, has blessed us.*

*May God continue to bless us;*

*let all the ends of the earth revere him.*

FROM PSALM 67

*We thank you for your gifts, merciful God,*

*and we ask you to give all people the food they need.*

*May we all be united one day*

*in the eternal singing of your praises,*

*through Christ, our Lord.*

*Amen.*

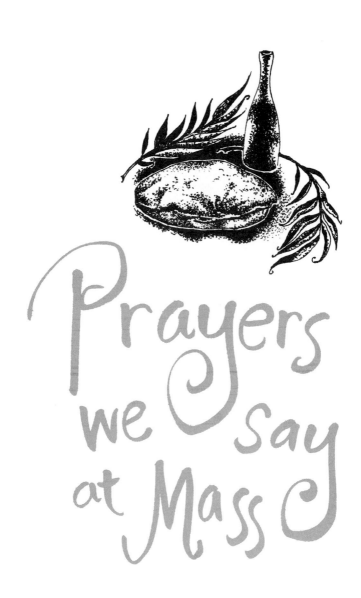

# Prayers we say at Mass

chapter four

# After years of Mass

attendance, we know certain prayers by heart. We may not remember where we first heard them or how we learned them, but they are a permanent part of our Catholic heritage. Children enjoy learning these prayers and saying them along with the grown-ups at Mass. Old people with failing memories can still say them without hesitation. And these prayers do not have to be reserved for Sundays. They are beautiful prayers for any time, any place.[8]

# Greeting

At the Beginning of Mass and the
Eucharistic Prayer:

PRIEST:

*The Lord be with you.*

RESPONSE:

*And also with you.*

## During Communion:

PRIEST:

*The peace of the Lord be with you always.*

RESPONSE:

*And also with you.*

The peace
of the Lord
be with you
always.

# Confiteor

Our sins and mistakes are not private affairs. They affect the whole family, the entire community. That is why we confess them to our brothers and sisters—at home or at church—as well as to God.

*I confess to almighty God*
*and to you, my brothers and sisters,*
*that I have sinned through my own fault,*
*in my thoughts and in my words,*
*in what I have done,*
*and in what I have failed to do.*
*And I ask blessed Mary, ever virgin,*
*all the angels and saints,*
*and you, my brothers and sisters,*
*to pray for me to the Lord our God.*

# Gloria

This ancient hymn of praise begins with the words of the angels who sang to shepherds in the hills of Bethlehem when Christ was born.

*Glory to God in the highest,*

*and peace to his people on earth.*

*Lord God, heavenly King,*

*almighty God and Father,*

*we worship you, we give you thanks,*

*we praise you for your glory.*

*Lord Jesus Christ, only Son of the Father,*

*Lord God, Lamb of God,*

*you take away the sin of the world:*

*have mercy on us;*

*you are seated at the right hand of the Father:*

*receive our prayer.*

*For you alone are the Holy One,*

*you alone are the Lord,*

*you alone are the Most High,*

> *Jesus Christ,*

> *with the Holy Spirit,*

> *in the glory of God the Father. Amen.*

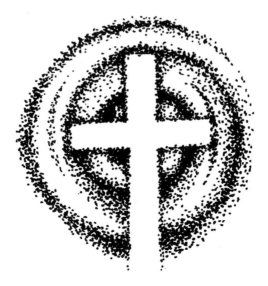

# The Nicene Creed

Throughout the history of the church, Christians have professed their faith by learning and reciting creeds, summary statements of faith that express the beliefs of the whole community. The Nicene Creed, whose roots are over sixteen hundred years old, describes the God we worship. Together we can pray it as an expression of faith and praise.

*We believe in one God,*
> *the Father, the Almighty,*
> *maker of heaven and earth,*
> *of all that is seen and unseen.*

*We believe in one Lord, Jesus Christ,*
> *the only Son of God,*
> *eternally begotten of the Father,*
> *God from God, Light from Light,*

*true God from true God,*

*begotten, not made, one in Being with the Father.*

*Through him all things were made.*

*For us men and for our salvation*

    *he came down from heaven:*

*by the power of the Holy Spirit*

    *he was born of the Virgin Mary, and*

        *became man.*

*For our sake he was crucified under Pontius*

        *Pilate;*

    *he suffered, died, and was buried.*

    *On the third day he rose again*

        *in fulfillment of the Scriptures;*

    *he ascended into heaven*

        *and is seated at the right hand of*

            *the Father.*

He will come again in glory to judge the living
and the dead,
and his kingdom will have no end.

We believe in the Holy Spirit, the Lord, the giver
of life,
who proceeds from the Father and the Son.
With the Father and the Son he is worshiped
and glorified.
He has spoken through the Prophets.
We believe in one holy catholic and apostolic
Church.
We acknowledge one baptism for the forgiveness
of sins.
We look for the resurrection of the dead,
and the life of the world to come. Amen.

Heaven and earth
are full of your
glory.

# Sanctus

One of the oldest Christian prayers, the Sanctus reminds us of the people who spread palm branches before Jesus as he rode into Jerusalem on the back of a donkey. "Hosanna!"—"Save us!"—they called out to him. The threefold repetition of "Holy" is in honor of the Trinity.

*Holy, holy, holy Lord, God of power and might,*
*heaven and earth are full of your glory.*
> *Hosanna in the highest.*
*Blessed is he who comes in the name of the Lord.*
> *Hosanna in the highest.*

# The Mystery of Faith

After the priest has consecrated the bread and wine, we all together affirm our faith in Christ's death, resurrection, and second coming. These short creeds can be prayed whenever we feel the need for added strength and courage.

## A

*Christ has died,*
*Christ is risen,*
*Christ will come again.*

## B

*Dying you destroyed our death,*
*rising you restored our life.*
*Lord Jesus, come in glory.*

## C

*When we eat this bread and drink this cup,*

*we proclaim your death, Lord Jesus,*

*until you come in glory.*

## D

*Lord, by your cross and resurrection*

*you have set us free.*

*You are the Savior of the world.*

# Agnus Dei

Often set to music, this prayer is addressed to Jesus the Lamb, the sacrifice whose death brings peace to the world.

*Lamb of God, you take away the sins of the world:*
*have mercy on us.*
*Lamb of God, you take away the sins of the world:*
*have mercy on us.*
*Lamb of God, you take away the sins of the world:*
*grant us peace.*

# Morning and Evening Prayer

chapter five

**M**arking the time of day with prayer is an ancient tradition in the church. For centuries monastics have kept the Divine Office, also known as the Liturgy of the Hours. The Divine Office focuses on praising God through praying psalms, canticles (short hymns that appear within scriptural texts), intercessions, and the Lord's Prayer. *The Constitution on the Sacred Liturgy* states that, in addition to clerics, "the laity, too, are encouraged to recite the Divine Office, either with the priests, or among themselves, or even individually."

The problem for many of us is that the Divine Office is complicated. It involves singing all the Psalms once each month, reading major portions of scripture each year, and meditating on inspirational writings of the saints. The full form of the Liturgy of the Hours requires several volumes of prayers, readings, and instructions. Most families don't have time for that, so several publishers have prepared shorter forms for family use.

If your family would like to try Morning and Evening Prayer, here is a model you can follow. It is based on Sunday of Week I of the Four-Week Psalter. Once you're comfortable with the rhythm, you may want to buy a more complete form of the Divine Office, such as *Shorter Christian Prayer* (New York: Catholic Book Publishing Co., 1988), from which these prayers were taken.

# Morning Prayer

Morning prayer is a wonderful way to get acquainted with the Liturgy of the Hours. Here is a simple form of Morning Prayer that families or individuals can use.

## Opening Prayers

*God, come to my assistance.*

*—Lord, make haste to help me.*

*Glory to the Father, and to the Son, and to the Holy Spirit:*

*as it was in the beginning, is now, and will be for ever. Amen (alleluia).*[9]

*As morning breaks I look to you, O God, to be my strength this day (alleluia).*[10]

Glory to the
Father,
and to the Son,
and to the
Holy Spirit:
as it was
in the beginning,
is now,
and will be
for ever.

# Psalm

A psalm is a song, and this is a lovely song to greet the day. After you know it well, you may wish to substitute other psalms. One person can read the entire psalm, or two people (or groups) can read alternate lines. If you choose to read alternate lines, notice how the second line usually repeats or completes the thought expressed in the first line. This repetition is typical of Hebrew songs and poems.

*O God, you are my God, I seek you,*
  *my soul thirsts for you;*
*my flesh faints for you,*
  *as in a dry and weary land where there is*
      *no water.*
*So I have looked upon you in the sanctuary,*

*beholding your power and glory.*

*Because your steadfast love is better than life,*

*my lips will praise you.*

*So I will bless you as long as I live;*

*I will lift up my hands and call on your name.*

*My soul is satisfied as with a rich feast,*

*and my mouth praises you with joyful lips*

*when I think of you on my bed,*

*and meditate on you in the watches of the night;*

*for you have been my help,*

*and in the shadow of your wings I sing for joy.*

*My soul clings to you;*

*your right hand upholds me.*

PSALM 63:1–8


*Glory to the Father . . .*

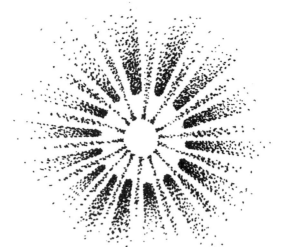

May our lips
praise you;
our lives
proclaim your
goodness.

## Psalm-prayer

*Father, creator of unfailing light, give that same light to those who call to you. May our lips praise you; our lives proclaim your goodness; our works give you honor, and our voices celebrate you for ever.*[11]

# A Reading from Scripture

Read a short passage of scripture of your choice. Some families use the daily readings (you can find them in a weekday missal or possibly in your parish bulletin) and some choose a book of the Bible to read straight through, a paragraph or two a day. Children often prefer the books of scripture that tell stories, including

> The Book of Genesis
>
> The Book of Ruth
>
> The Book of Judith

The Book of Esther

The Book of Daniel

The Gospel according to Matthew

The Gospel according to Mark

The Gospel according to Luke

The Gospel according to John

The Acts of the Apostles

# Canticle of Zechariah

This is the prayer of the priest Zechariah at the birth of his son, John, now known as John the Baptizer.

*Blessed be the Lord, the God of Israel;*
*he has come to his people and set them free.*

*He has raised up for us a mighty savior,*
*born of the house of his servant David.*

*Through his holy prophets he promised of old*
*that he would save us from our enemies,*
*from the hands of all who hate us.*

*He promised to show mercy to our fathers*
*and to remember his holy covenant.*

*This was the oath he swore to our father Abraham:*
*to set us free from the hands of our enemies,*
*free to worship him without fear,*
*holy and righteous in his sight*
*all the days of our life.*

*You, my child, shall be called the prophet of the*
*Most High,*
*for you will go before the Lord to prepare his way,*
*to give his people knowledge of salvation*
*by the forgiveness of their sins.*

*In the tender compassion of our God*

*the dawn from on high shall break upon us,*

*to shine on those who dwell in darkness and the*

*shadow of death,*

*and to guide our feet into the way of peace.*[12]

## Intercessions

Family members share their prayer intentions.
After each spoken concern, the family says:

*Lord, hear our prayer.*

When all have had a chance to pray, the family
prays together:

*Our Father . . .*

## Closing Prayer and Blessing

The family says together:

*Almighty and ever-present Father,*

*your watchful care reaches from end to end*
*and orders all things in such power*
*that even the tensions and the tragedies of sin*
*cannot frustrate your loving plans.*
*Help us to embrace your will,*
*give us the strength to follow your call,*
*so that your truth may live in our hearts*
*and reflect peace to those who believe in your love.*
*We ask this in the name of Jesus the Lord.*

The leader says, as all make the sign of the cross:

*May the Lord bless us,*
*protect us from all evil*
*and bring us to everlasting life.*

*Amen.*[13]

# Evening Prayer

Right after dinner or just before bedtime, the family gathers and turns their thoughts toward God.

## Opening Prayers

*God, come to my assistance.*

*—Lord, make haste to help me.*

*Glory to the Father, and to the Son, and to the*
*    Holy Spirit:*
*as it was in the beginning, is now, and will be*
*    for ever. Amen (alleluia).[14]*

*Like burning incense, Lord, let my prayer rise up*
*to you (alleluia).[15]*

# Psalm

At the end of a busy day, this psalm, or song, expresses our trust in God. Read it in unison, or divide into two groups and read alternate lines. After you know it well, you may wish to substitute other psalms.

*I call upon you, O Lord; come quickly to me;*
*give ear to my voice when I call to you.*
*Let my prayer be counted as incense before you,*
*and the lifting up of my hands as an evening*
     *sacrifice.*
*Set a guard over my mouth, O Lord;*
*keep watch over the door of my lips.*
*Do not turn my heart to any evil,*
*to busy myself with wicked deeds*
*in company with those who work iniquity;*

*do not let me eat of their delicacies.*

*My eyes are turned toward you, O God, my Lord;*

*in you I seek refuge; do not leave me defenseless.*

PSALM 141:1–4, 8


*Glory to the Father . . .*

## Psalm-prayer

*Lord, from the rising of the sun to its setting your name is worthy of all praise. Let our prayer come like incense before you. May the lifting up of our hands be as an evening sacrifice acceptable to you, Lord our God.*[16]

# A Reading from Scripture

Read a short passage of scripture of your choice. Some families use the daily readings (you can find them in a weekday missal or possibly in your parish bulletin) and some choose favorite selections such as

> Isaiah 40: "Comfort, O comfort
>     my people"
>
> Isaiah 55: "Come to the waters"
>
> John 5:22–59: The Bread from Heaven
>
> John 14: "Do not let your hearts
>     be troubled"
>
> Romans 8:31–39: God's Love for Us
>
> 1 Corinthians 13: The Love Chapter

# The Canticle of Mary

When Mary learned she would be the mother of our Lord, she went to visit her relative Elizabeth, who was soon to become the mother of John the Baptizer. This song of praise, also known as the Magnificat, is Mary's response to Elizabeth's greeting.

*My soul proclaims the greatness of the Lord,*
*my spirit rejoices in God my Savior;*
*for he has looked with favor on his lowly servant.*

*From this day all generations will call me blessed:*
*the Almighty has done great things for me,*
*and holy is his Name.*

*He has mercy on those who fear him*
*in every generation.*

*He has shown the strength of his arm,*
*he has scattered the proud in their conceit.*

*He has cast down the mighty from their thrones,*
*and has lifted up the lowly.*

*He has filled the hungry with good things,*
*and the rich he has sent away empty.*

*He has come to the help of his servant Israel*
*for he has remembered his promise of mercy,*
*the promise he made to our fathers,*
*to Abraham and his children for ever.*[17]

# Intercessions

Family members share their prayer intentions.
After each spoken concern, the family says:

*Lord, hear our prayer.*

When all have had a chance to pray, the family
prays together:

*Our Father . . .*

# Lord, hear our prayer.

# Closing Prayer and Blessing

The family says together:

*Father of love,*

*hear our prayers.*

*Help us to know your will*

*and to do it with courage and faith.*

*Grant this through our Lord Jesus Christ, your Son,*

*who lives and reigns with you and the Holy Spirit,*

*one God, for ever and ever.*

The leader says, as all make the sign of the cross:

*May the Lord bless us,*

*protect us from all evil*

*and bring us to everlasting life.*

*Amen.*[18]

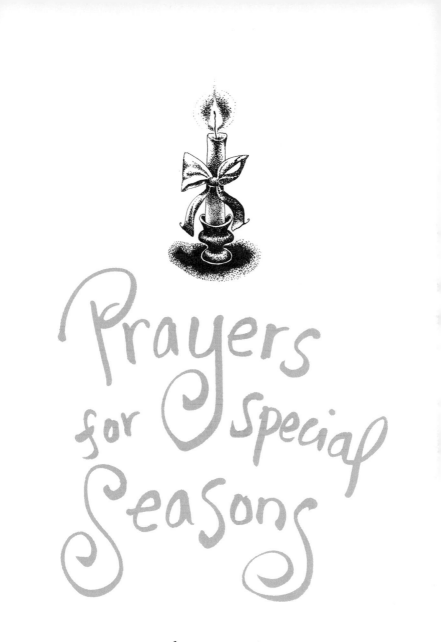

# Prayers for special Seasons

chapter six

Catholic worship and celebration follow a yearly cycle known as the liturgical year. Catholics—along with many other Christians around the world—follow this seasonal calendar by observing Advent, Christmas, Lent, Easter, and Ordinary Time. Much can be done at home to connect family prayer with the prayer cycle of the church. Because holy days and holidays frequently coincide, these are particularly good times to create family prayer traditions.

Put candles, flowers, or decorative cloths in your family's prayer space, and change the colors to match the seasons: violet for Advent, white for Christmas, violet for Lent, white for Easter, red for Pentecost, and green for Ordinary Time. Use prayer models to help celebrate the seasons of the church year. Here are just a few suggestions.

# Advent

The liturgical year begins with Advent, a word derived from Latin that means "coming." The Advent season includes the four weeks before Christmas, beginning with the Sunday on or closest to November 30 and ending Christmas Eve. During Advent we prepare to celebrate the birth of Christ, and we look forward to Christ's second coming at the end of time. The liturgical color for Advent is violet.

## The Advent Wreath

The Advent wreath is a popular family devotion for this season. It is usually a circle of evergreen branches surrounding four candles, one for each of the Sundays of Advent. Frequently, three of the candles are violet and one is rose. The rose-colored candle is lit during the third week of Advent, beginning on Gaudete Sunday (*gaudete* means "joyful") as a reminder that our waiting will soon be over.

The Advent wreath is blessed on the first Sunday of Advent. One candle is lit the first week, two the second week, three the third week, and all four the fourth week. The prayer text for each week comes from the opening prayer for that Sunday's Mass. An Advent hymn and scripture reading may be included. For younger children, the prayers for each week may be simplified. Here is a good Advent prayer for all ages.

*Come, Lord Jesus, we are waiting for your birthday.*

# Blessing the Advent Wreath

On the first Sunday of Advent, gather the family and bless the Advent wreath. Begin by making the sign of the cross.

LEADER:

*Our help is in the name of the Lord.*

ALL:

*Who made heaven and earth.*

## Reading

*The people who walked in darkness*
*have seen a great light;*
*those who lived in a land of deep darkness—*
*on them light has shined.*
*You have multiplied the nation,*
*you have increased its joy;*

*they rejoice before you*

*as with joy at the harvest,*

*as people exult when dividing plunder.*

*For a child has been born for us,*

*a son given to us;*

*authority rests upon his shoulders;*

*and he is named*

*Wonderful Counselor, Mighty God,*

*Everlasting Father, Prince of Peace.*

*His authority shall grow continually,*

*and there shall be endless peace*

*for the throne of David and his kingdom.*

*He will establish and uphold it*

*with justice and with righteousness*

*from this time onward and for evermore.*

*The zeal of the Lord of hosts will do this.*

ISAIAH 9:2–3, 6–7

# Blessing

A parent leads the family in one of these blessings, or the family prays it in unison.

*Lord God,*
*your Church joyfully awaits the coming of its Savior,*
*who enlightens our hearts*
*and dispels the darkness of ignorance and sin.*

*Pour forth your blessings upon us*
*as we light the candles of this wreath;*
*may their light reflect the splendor of Christ,*
*who is Lord, for ever and ever.*

*Amen.*

Or the family prays:

*Lord our God,*

*we praise you for your Son, Jesus Christ:*

*he is Emmanuel, the hope of the peoples,*

*he is the wisdom that teaches and guides us,*

*he is the Savior of every nation.*

*Lord God,*

*let your blessing come upon us*

*as we light the candles of this wreath.*

*May the wreath and its light*

*be a sign of Christ's promise to bring us salvation.*

*May he come quickly and not delay.*

*We ask this through Christ our Lord.*

*Amen.*[19]

Pour forth
your blessings
upon us
as we light
the candles
of this wreath.

# The First Week of Advent

This ceremony is meant for every day during the first week of Advent, beginning with the first Sunday.[20]

The family prays one of these prayers as the first candle is lighted.

*All-powerful God,*
*increase our strength of will for doing good*
*that Christ may find an eager welcome at his coming*
*and call us to his side in the kingdom of heaven,*
*where he lives and reigns with you and the Holy*
    *Spirit,*
*one God, for ever and ever.*

*Amen.*

Or the family prays:

*Father in heaven,*
*our hearts desire the warmth of your love,*
*and our minds are searching for the light of your*
    *Word.*

*Increase our longing for Christ our Savior*
*and give us the strength to grow in love,*
*that the dawn of his coming may find us rejoicing in*
    *his presence*
*and welcoming the light of his truth.*

*We ask this in the name of Jesus the Lord.*

*Amen.*

# The Second Week of Advent

The family prays one of these prayers as two candles are lighted.

*God of power and mercy,*
*open our hearts in welcome.*
*Remove the things that hinder us from receiving*
    *Christ with joy,*
*so that we may share his wisdom*
*and become one with him*
*when he comes in glory,*
*for he lives and reigns with you and the Holy Spirit,*
*one God, for ever and ever.*

*Amen.*

May the darkness
not blind us.

Or the family prays:

*Father in heaven,*

*the day draws near when the glory of your Son*

*will make radiant the night of the waiting world.*

*May the lure of greed not impede us from the joy*

*which moves the hearts of those who seek him.*

*May the darkness not blind us*

*to the vision of wisdom*

*which fills the minds of those who find him.*

*We ask this in the name of Jesus the Lord.*

*Amen.*

# The Third Week of Advent

The family prays one of these prayers as three candles, including the rose-colored one, are lighted.

*Lord God,*
*may we, your people,*
*who look forward to the birthday of Christ,*
*experience the joy of salvation*
*and celebrate that feast with love and thanksgiving.*

*We ask this through our Lord Jesus Christ, your Son,*
*who lives and reigns with you and the Holy Spirit,*
*one God, for ever and ever.*

*Amen.*

Or the family prays:

*Father of our Lord Jesus Christ,*
*ever faithful to your promises*
*and ever close to your Church:*
*the earth rejoices in hope of the Savior's coming*
*and looks forward with longing*
*to his return at the end of time.*

*Prepare our hearts and remove the sadness*
*that hinders us from feeling the joy and hope*
*which his presence will bestow,*
*for he is Lord for ever and ever.*

*Amen.*

# The Fourth Week of Advent

The family prays one of these prayers as all four candles are lighted.

*Lord,*
*fill our hearts with your love,*
*and as you revealed to us by an angel*
*the coming of your Son as man,*
*so lead us through his suffering and death*
*to the glory of his resurrection,*
*for he lives and reigns with you and the Holy Spirit,*
*one God, for ever and ever.*

*Amen.*

Or the family prays:

*Father, all-powerful God,*
*your eternal Word took flesh on our earth*
*when the Virgin Mary placed her life*
*at the service of your plan.*

*Lift our minds in watchful hope*
*to hear the voice which announces his glory,*
*and open our minds to receive the Spirit*
*who prepares us for his coming.*

*We ask this through Christ our Lord.*

*Amen.*

# Christmas

Christmas, the memorial of Christ's birth, is celebrated December 25. Christmas is also a full liturgical season extending from the vigil of Christmas (Christmas Eve) to the Feast of the Baptism of the Lord, celebrated the Sunday after January 6. Included within the Christmas season are many celebrations that recall the early life of Jesus:

the Feast of the Holy Innocents

　　(December 28)

the Feast of the Holy Family

　　(the Sunday after Christmas)

the Solemnity of Mary, Mother of God

　　(January 1)

the Solemnity of Epiphany

　　(January 6, or the Sunday occurring

　　between January 2 and 8)

The liturgical color for the Christmas season
is white.

Here are some Christmas traditions you may
want to use in your family's prayer time.

# Blessing the Christmas Manger

St. Francis of Assisi introduced the custom of displaying the Christmas manger, also called the Nativity scene or crèche. If you have a Christmas manger in your home, you may wish to bless it. Some families set up the Nativity scene on Christmas Eve. Others set it up earlier in Advent but do not put the infant Jesus in the manger until Christmas Eve or Christmas Day.

Gather the family around the Christmas manger and make the sign of the cross.

LEADER:

*Our help is in the name of the Lord.*

ALL:

*Who made heaven and earth.*

## Reading

In those days a decree went out from Emperor Augustus that all the world should be registered. This was the first registration and was taken while Quirinius was governor of Syria. All went to their own towns to be registered. Joseph also went from the town of Nazareth in Galilee to Judea, to the city of David called Bethlehem, because he was descended from the house and family of David. He went to be registered with Mary, to whom he was engaged and who was expecting a child. While they were there, the time came for her to deliver her child. And she gave birth to her firstborn son and wrapped him in bands of cloth, and laid him in a manger, because there was no place for them in the inn.

LUKE 2:1–7

## Blessing Prayer

A parent leads, or the family prays in unison.

*God of every nation and people,*
*from the very beginning of creation*
*you have made manifest your love:*
*when our need for a Savior was great*
*you sent your Son to be born of the Virgin Mary.*
*To our lives he brings joy and peace,*
*justice, mercy, and love.*

*Lord,*
*bless all who look upon this manger;*
*may it remind us of the humble birth of Jesus,*
*and raise up our thoughts to him,*
*who is God-with-us and Savior of all,*
*and who lives and reigns for ever and ever.*

*Amen.*[21]

To our lives
he brings joy
and peace,
justice, mercy,
and love.

# Blessing the Christmas Tree

Traditionally, families set up the Christmas tree on Christmas Eve and kept it up until the Solemnity of Epiphany. It was a festivity that belonged to the Christmas season, not to Advent. If your family prefers to decorate the tree earlier, you might try waiting to turn on the tree lights until after the prayer of blessing on Christmas Eve.

Gather the family around the Christmas tree and make the sign of the cross.

LEADER:

*Blessed be the name of the Lord.*

ALL:

*Now and for ever.*

## Reading

In the beginning was the Word, and the Word was with God, and the Word was God. He was in the beginning with God. All things came into being through him, and without him not one thing came into being. What has come into being in him was life, and the life was the light of all people. The light shines in the darkness, and the darkness did not overcome it.

JOHN 1:1–5

## Blessing Prayer

A parent leads, or the family prays one of these prayers in unison.

*Lord our God,*

*we praise you for the light of creation:*

*the sun, the moon, and the stars of the night.*

We praise you for the light of Israel:

the Law, the prophets, and the wisdom of the
   Scriptures.

We praise you for Jesus Christ, your Son:

he is Emmanuel, God-with-us, the Prince of Peace,

who fills us with the wonder of your love.

Lord God,

let your blessing come upon us

as we illumine this tree.

May the light and cheer it gives

be a sign of the joy that fills our hearts.

May all who delight in this tree

come to the knowledge and joy of salvation.

We ask this through Christ our Lord.

Amen.[22]

Or the family prays:

*Holy Lord,*
*we come with joy to celebrate the birth of your Son,*
*who rescued us from the darkness of sin*
*by making the cross a tree of life and light.*

*May this tree, arrayed in splendor,*
*remind us of the life-giving cross of Christ,*
*that we may always rejoice*
*in the new life that shines in our hearts.*

*We ask this through Christ our Lord.*

*Amen.*

Light the Christmas tree. Sing Christmas hymns and carols. Keep the feast. Christ is born!

# Lent

Lent is the name given to the time of preparation for Easter, lasting about forty days in honor of Christ's forty-day temptation in the wilderness. Lent begins on Ash Wednesday, when the sign of the cross is marked on our foreheads in ashes. It continues until the Thursday before Easter, when we celebrate the Mass of the Lord's Supper. Six Sundays are included in Lent. The sixth Sunday is called Passion or Palm Sunday and marks the beginning of Holy Week. The liturgical color for Lent is violet.

The themes of Lent include both penance and baptism, as we recall Christ's suffering and journey with those preparing for initiation into the church. During this season, the word "alleluia" is not said during Mass or in Catholic prayer. "Alleluia!" will return as the refrain of praise at Easter and throughout the Easter season.

The Jesus Prayer, beloved by Christians in the East, is an excellent prayer for the whole family to say throughout Lent.

*Lord Jesus Christ,*
*Son of God,*
*have mercy on me,*
*a sinner.*

# Praying by Our Actions

During Lent, the church calls us to penance—sorrow for our sins. Several traditional disciplines help us to repent. We can offer these actions as prayers to God, because through them we resolve to conform our lives to Christ.

> Fasting and abstinence on Ash
> Wednesday and Good Friday
> Abstaining from meat on Fridays
> during Lent
> Celebrating the Sacrament of
> Reconciliation
> Almsgiving: sharing our material resources
> with the poor

Many Catholics practice a voluntary fast during Lent by giving up something they normally enjoy. Families can decide together on additional practices, such as giving up television one night of the week. Or they might decide to forgo eating out and give the money they would have spent to charitable organizations, such as Catholic Relief Services' Operation Rice Bowl. During Lent, families can be especially attentive to their prayer times, perhaps adding reading scripture to their daily routines.

All of these practices are meant to remind us of our need for God's forgiveness and to lead us to greater fervor in the Christian life.

# Act of Contrition

Lent is the time of year for searching our souls, feeling sorrow for our sins, asking forgiveness of God and those we have hurt, and determining to do better. It is a usual time to celebrate the Sacrament of Reconciliation.

There are many ways we sin against God, and there are many ways we can call to God for forgiveness. An Act of Contrition is a prayer in which we confess our sinfulness to God and ask for God's forgiveness. Catholics are encouraged to pray an Act of Contrition every day. We also pray an Act of Contrition as part of the Sacrament of Reconciliation. Here is a traditional Act of Contrition.

*My God,*

*I am sorry for my sins with all my heart.*

*In choosing to do wrong*

*and failing to do good,*

*I have sinned against you*

*whom I should love above all things.*

*I firmly intend, with your help,*

*to do penance,*

*to sin no more,*

*and to avoid whatever leads me to sin.*

*Our Savior Jesus Christ*

*suffered and died for us.*

*In his name, my God, have mercy.*[23]

# The Stations of the Cross

This popular devotion recalls the events of Christ's last day. It is probably based on the visits made by pilgrims to the Holy Land who walked the route Christ followed on his way to death. Pictorial representations for each station can be found in almost all Catholic churches. These stations provide the faithful with an aid in praying this devotion; however, stations are not necessary. It is particularly popular to pray the Stations of the Cross during Lent, especially on Fridays in commemoration of Christ's death on that day of the week.

The following is a list of the Stations of the Cross with short scripture passages. Not all the stations can be found in the Passion stories of the Gospels; some are based on pious tradition.

## First Station:
## Jesus is condemned to death

Then the people as a whole answered, "His blood be on us and on our children!" So . . . after flogging Jesus, [Pilate] handed him over to be crucified.

MATTHEW 27:25–26

## Second Station:
## Jesus accepts his cross

After mocking him, [the soldiers of the governor] stripped him of the robe and put his own clothes on him. Then they led him away to crucify him.

MATTHEW 27:31

# Third Station:
# Jesus falls the first time

I gave my back to those who struck me, and my cheeks to those who pulled out the beard; I did not hide my face from insult and spitting.

ISAIAH 50:6

# Fourth Station:
# Jesus meets his mother

Simeon blessed them and said to his mother Mary, "This child is destined for the falling and the rising of many in Israel, and to be a sign that will be opposed so that the inner thoughts of many will be revealed—and a sword will pierce your own soul too."

LUKE 2:34–35

## Fifth Station:
## Simon helps Jesus carry the cross

As they went out, they came upon a man from Cyrene named Simon; they compelled this man to carry his cross.

MATTHEW 27:32

## Sixth Station:
## Veronica wipes the face of Jesus

And the soldiers wove a crown of thorns and put it on his head, and they dressed him in a purple robe. They kept coming up to him, saying, "Hail, King of the Jews!" and striking him on the face.

JOHN 19:2–3

## Seventh Station:
## Jesus falls the second time

Surely he has borne our infirmities and carried our diseases; yet we accounted him stricken, struck down by God, and afflicted.

ISAIAH 53:4

## Eighth Station:
## Jesus speaks to the weeping women

"Daughters of Jerusalem, do not weep for me, but weep for yourselves and for your children."

LUKE 23:28

## Ninth Station:
## Jesus falls the third time

But he was wounded for our transgressions, crushed for our iniquities; upon him was the punishment that made us whole.

ISAIAH 53:5

## Tenth Station:
## Jesus is stripped of his garments

They stare and gloat over me; they divide my clothes among themselves, and for my clothing they cast lots.

PSALM 22:17–18

## Eleventh Station:
## Jesus is nailed to the cross

Then Jesus said, "Father, forgive them; for they do not know what they are doing."

LUKE 23:34

## Twelfth Station:
## Jesus dies on the cross

Then Jesus cried again with a loud voice and breathed his last.

MATTHEW 27:50

## Thirteenth Station:
## Jesus is taken down from the cross

After these things, Joseph of Arimathea, who was a disciple of Jesus, though a secret one, . . . asked Pilate to let him take away the body of Jesus. Pilate gave his permission; so he came and removed his body.

JOHN 19:38

## Fourteenth Station:
## Jesus is buried

Joseph took the body and wrapped it in a clean linen cloth and laid it in his own new tomb, which he had hewn in the rock. He then rolled a great stone to the door of the tomb and went away.

MATTHEW 27:59–60

## Epilogue: The Resurrection

Was it not necessary that the Messiah should suffer these things and then enter into his glory?

LUKE 24:26

# Easter Triduum

Between Lent and Easter Sunday lie the three most important days in the church calendar. These are Holy Thursday, Good Friday, and Holy Saturday. On these three days the church gathers to commemorate the passion (suffering), death, and resurrection of Jesus.

On Holy Thursday, we celebrate the Mass of the Lord's Supper, during which we recall Jesus' Last Supper with his disciples and do as he did by washing one another's feet.

On Good Friday, we gather to commemorate the Lord's passion. This is the only day in the church year when no Mass is celebrated. Instead, when we gather to venerate the cross, we share Eucharist that has been consecrated at Thursday's Mass of the Lord's Supper.

The Triduum culminates in the celebration of the Easter Vigil on Holy Saturday. We gather in darkness to await the resurrection of Christ. If there are adults and older children in the community who are to be baptized, their baptism, confirmation, and first Eucharist are celebrated at the Vigil. All of the faithful are encouraged to observe the Easter fast, which extends the Good Friday fast through Holy Saturday, until the Easter Vigil.

Families who choose to attend all the Easter Triduum services will experience the fullness of our Easter celebration. Families might also pray the Stations of the Cross on Good Friday. Then, at the Easter Vigil, the festivity begins. This spirit of joy can continue at home with a "break-the-fast" meal immediately after the Vigil.

# Easter

Easter is the most important feast day in the church year. It is the day on which we celebrate Christ's resurrection from the dead. Like Christmas, Easter is both a day and a season. The season of Easter extends for fifty days, beginning on Easter Sunday and ending on Pentecost. The fortieth day after Easter is the Feast of the Ascension, a holy day of obligation.

Eastertide—all fifty days of it—is considered one great Sunday. The liturgical color for the Easter season is white. A good family prayer for Easter is the ancient exclamation of praise to God:

*Alleluia!*

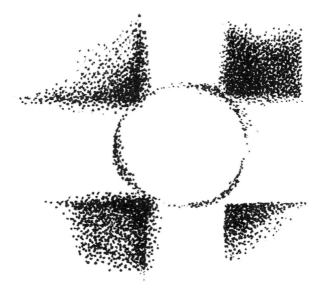

Alleluia!

# Blessing of Food for the First Meal of Easter

For people who fast during Lent and especially during Good Friday and Holy Saturday, the first meal of Easter is especially welcome. Thus it has become customary to bless this meal in a special way. Here is a suggestion for celebrating this ritual.

LEADER:

*Christ is risen. Alleluia.*

ALL:

*He is risen indeed. Alleluia.*

He is
risen
indeed.

## Reading

Now on that same day two of them were going to a village called Emmaus, about seven miles from Jerusalem, and talking with each other about all these things that had happened. While they were talking and discussing, Jesus himself came near and went with them, but their eyes were kept from recognizing him. And he said to them, "What are you discussing with each other while you walk along?" They stood still, looking sad. Then one of them, whose name was Cleopas, answered him, "Are you the only stranger in Jerusalem who does not know the things that have taken place there in these days?" He asked them, "What things?" They replied, "The things about Jesus of Nazareth, who was a prophet mighty in deed and word before God and all the people, and how our chief priests and leaders handed him over to be condemned to death and crucified him. But we had hoped that he was the one to redeem Israel. Yes, and besides all this, it is now the third day since these things took place. Moreover, some women of our group astounded us. They were at the tomb early this morning, and when they did not find his body there, they came back and told us that they had indeed seen a vision of angels who said that he was alive. Some of those who were with us went to the tomb and found it just as the women had said; but they did not see him." Then he said to them, "Oh, how foolish you are, and how slow of heart to believe all that the prophets have declared! Was it not necessary that the Messiah should suffer these things and then enter into his glory?" Then beginning with Moses and all the prophets, he interpreted to them the things about himself in all the scriptures.

As they came near the village to which they were going, he walked ahead as if he were going on. But they urged him strongly, saying, "Stay with us, because it is almost evening and the day is now nearly over." So he went in to stay with them. When he was at the table with them, he took bread, blessed and broke it, and gave it to them. Then their eyes were opened, and they recognized him; and he vanished from their sight. They said to each other, "Were not our hearts burning within us while he was talking to us on the road, while he was opening the scriptures to us?" That same hour they got up and returned to Jerusalem; and they found the eleven and their companions gathered together. They were saying, "The Lord has risen indeed, and he has appeared to Simon!" Then they told what had happened on the road, and how he had been made known to them in the breaking of the bread.

LUKE 24:13–35

# Blessing Prayer

A parent can lead this prayer, or the family can pray in unison.

*God of glory,*
*the eyes of all turn to you*
*as we celebrate Christ's victory over sin and death.*
*Bless us and this food of our first Easter meal.*
*May we who gather at the Lord's table*
*continue to celebrate the joy of his resurrection*
*and be admitted finally to his heavenly banquet.*

*Grant this through Christ our Lord.*

*Amen.*[24]

## Prayer during the Easter Season

Easter, like Lent, is a time for prayer. In Lent we searched our souls and prayed for God's mercy. Now in Eastertide we rejoice and praise God. This is a wonderful season to begin following the weekday cycle of readings for Mass. Families can gather throughout the fifty days of the Easter season to read scripture and pray joyful

Alleluias. Here are some praises designated for the Monday following Easter Sunday.

*The Lord has risen from the dead, as he foretold. Let there be happiness and rejoicing, for he is our King for ever. Alleluia!*

*This is the day the Lord has made; let us rejoice and be glad. Alleluia!*

*Christ now raised from the dead will never die again; death no longer has power over him. Alleluia!*

# Ordinary Time

Ordinary Time is the rest of the year—the time when no particular aspect of Christ's life is being celebrated. There is a period of Ordinary Time after the Christmas season and before Lent, and another, longer period after Pentecost until Advent. The liturgical color for Ordinary Time is green.

Ordinary Time is an ideal time for ordinary prayers. It is a good time to begin observing Morning and Evening Prayer. Here is a little prayer by the thirteenth-century saint Richard of Chichester, whose words inspired the *Godspell* song "Day by Day."

*Thanks be to you, O Lord Jesus Christ, for all the benefits you have given us,*

and for all the pains and insults you have borne
for us.
O most merciful redeemer, friend, and brother,
may we know you more clearly,
love you more dearly,
and follow you more nearly;
for your own sake.

Amen.

# Devotions to Mary

chapter seven

The Catholic church has always given Mary a place of special reverence. Not only is she honored as Mother of God, she is also called Mother of the Church and therefore Mother of us all. We revere her as a model of faith, humility, and courage.

Because of the many traditions of Mary's appearances and special miracles, many cultures have particular devotions to her. Included among these are Our Lady of Guadalupe (Mexico), Our Lady of Czestochowa (Poland), Our Lady of Lourdes (France), and Our Lady of Fatima (Portugal).

Though we love and respect Mary, we do not worship her. Worship is reserved for the Trinity. Our devotion to Mary leads us to greater union with God.

# The Hail Mary

This popular Marian prayer is based on words spoken to Mary in the Gospel of Luke—those spoken by the angel at the Annunciation, and those spoken by Elizabeth at the Visitation. This prayer is prayed repeatedly in the Rosary, a meditative Marian devotion during which we reflect on the Glorious, Joyful, and Sorrowful Mysteries of the life of Christ and of Mary.

Hail Mary,

full of grace,

the Lord is with you.

Blessed are you among women,

and blessed is the fruit of your womb, Jesus.

Holy Mary, Mother of God,

pray for us sinners

now and at the hour of our death.

Amen.

# The Rosary

The Rosary is one of the most popular Catholic devotions. Its rhythmic repetition helps us focus our thoughts and become aware of God's presence. The images of the three sets of Mysteries enrich our meditation on the life of Christ and Mary. People who pray the Rosary—whether individually or with the family—say it is a powerful tool in their spiritual life.

A rosary is a chain of beads set in groups of ten, called decades. Each bead represents a Hail Mary, and each decade represents a Mystery to be meditated on while reciting the prayers. Each decade is framed by a large bead, for the Lord's Prayer, and a space, for the Doxology.

A complete Rosary consists of praying fifteen decades while meditating on all fifteen Mysteries. However, most people select one of the three groups of five Mysteries and pray just five decades a day. Here is how to pray the Rosary:

Make the sign of the cross:

*In the name of the Father . . .*

While holding the crucifix of the rosary, recite the Apostles' Creed.

*I believe in one God . . .*

Move your fingers to the large bead next to the crucifix. While holding it, say the Lord's Prayer.

*Our Father . . .*

Grasp the first small bead and say a Hail Mary for the gift of faith. On the second small bead, say a Hail Mary for the gift of hope. And on the third small bead, say a Hail Mary for the gift of love.

*Hail Mary . . .*

Slide your fingers to the space following the third small bead, and say the Doxology.

*Glory to the Father . . .*

Slide your finger to the large bead where the circle begins, and say the Lord's Prayer. You will say the Lord's Prayer at the beginning of each decade, every time your fingers meet a large bead.

*Our Father . . .*

Now you are ready to begin the first decade. Announce the Mystery on which you will meditate. For example, if you are saying the Joyful Mysteries, you will announce: "The Annunciation."

Take the each of the ten small beads in turn, each time saying a Hail Mary.

*Hail Mary . . .*

After the tenth bead, your fingers will encounter a space. Say the Doxology.

*Glory to the Father . . .*

You have now completed the first decade and the first Mystery. Announce the second Mystery: "The Visitation."

Repeat the cycle until you have meditated on all five Mysteries. (If this sounds complicated, just remember that the large beads are for the Our Father, the small beads are for the Hail Mary, and the spaces are for the Glory to the Father.) Many people conclude by praying the Salve Regina.

*Hail, holy Queen . . .*

# The Joyful Mysteries

Meditate on these scenes from the Gospels on Mondays and Thursdays and also on Sundays from Advent to the beginning of Lent.

## The Annunciation

Luke 1:26–38. The Archangel Gabriel appears to the Virgin Mary and tells her she will bear a son. Mary responds, "Here am I, the servant of the Lord; let it be with me according to your word."

## The Visitation

Luke 1:39–56. Mary visits her relative Elizabeth, who is pregnant with John the Baptizer. Mary prays the Magnificat: "My soul magnifies the Lord . . ."

## The Birth of Our Lord

Luke 2:1–20; Matthew 1:18–25. Mary and Joseph travel to Bethlehem, where Mary gives birth to Jesus in a stable. Meanwhile angels appear to shepherds and sing, "Glory to God in the highest heaven, and on earth peace among those whom he favors!"

## The Presentation of Jesus in the Temple

Luke 2:22–38. Mary and Joseph take Jesus to the temple for the ritual purification. Anna praises God and Simeon gives thanks: "My eyes have seen your salvation, which you have prepared in the presence of all peoples."

# The Finding of Jesus in the Temple

Luke 2:41–52. Returning to Galilee after Passover, Mary and Joseph lose sight of the twelve-year-old Jesus, who has stayed in Jerusalem to talk with the teachers. "Why were you searching for me?" he asks. "Did you not know that I must be in my Father's house?"

# The Sorrowful Mysteries

Reflect on these events in Christ's life on Tuesdays and Fridays, and also on the Sundays during Lent.

## The Agony in the Garden

Matthew 26:36–56; Mark 14:32–52; Luke 22:39–53; John 18:1–11. Knowing he will soon be killed, Jesus prays in great anguish while his disciples doze. Judas arrives with soldiers, who arrest Jesus.

## The Scourging at the Pillar

Matthew 27:26; Mark 14:65; 15:15; Luke 22:63–65; John 19:1. The soldiers strike Jesus, torment him, and spit on him. Pilate has Jesus flogged.

## The Crowning of Thorns

Matthew 27:27–31; Mark 15:16–20; John 19:2–3. The soldiers make a crown of thorns and place it on Jesus' head. They dress him in a purple robe and make fun of him, calling him "King of the Jews."

## The Carrying of the Cross

Matthew 27:32; Mark 15:21; Luke 23:26; John 19:16–17. Tradition says that Jesus attempted to carry his own cross but, weakened by loss of blood, stumbled under its weight. Simon of Cyrene is then asked to carry the cross for him.

## The Crucifixion and Death of Jesus

Matthew 27:33–66; Mark 15:22–47; Luke 23:32–56; John 19:18–42. Jesus is nailed to his cross, which is planted in the ground between two crucified thieves. He dies within hours, forgiving those who crucified him. Nicodemus and Joseph of Arimathea take him down from the cross and bury him in Joseph's tomb.

# The Glorious Mysteries

Rejoice in these triumphant moments on Wednesdays and Saturdays, and also on Sundays from Easter to Advent.

## The Resurrection

Matthew 28:1–10; Mark 16:1–13; Luke 24:1–49; John 20:1–29. Before daybreak Sunday morning, Jesus rises from the dead. He appears first to Mary Magdalene, then to Peter and John, the other disciples, and two followers on their way to Emmaus.

## The Ascension

Matthew 28:16–20; Mark 16:19–20; Luke 24:50–53; Acts 1:6–11. While his disciples watch, Jesus leaves this earth and is received into heaven, promising power from the Holy Spirit. Angels tell the disciples that Jesus will return.

## The Descent of the Holy Spirit

John 20:19–23; Acts 2:1–13. The disciples, along with Mary and other women, gather regularly for prayer. With the sound of a rushing wind and the appearance of fire, the Holy Spirit comes upon the group, who begin speaking in foreign languages.

## The Assumption of Mary into Heaven

Though scripture does not mention Mary's last days, tradition tells us she retired at St. John's home near Ephesus. There are no relics of Mary and no burial site because, when she died, she was taken body and soul to heaven.

# The Crowning of Mary as Queen of Heaven

Revelation 12:1. Mary is often likened to the woman in Revelation who is "clothed with the sun, with the moon under her feet, and on her head a crown of twelve stars."

# Queen of Heaven

The fourth Glorious Mystery of the Rosary celebrates Mary's assumption into heaven, and the fifth, her coronation. Thus one of the many titles given to Mary is "Queen of Heaven." Her queenship is celebrated as a memorial August 22, one week after the Solemnity of the Assumption. This prayer was composed in the twelfth century.

ALL:

*Queen of heaven, rejoice, alleluia.*

> *For Christ, your Son and Son of God,*
> *has risen as he said, alleluia.*
> *Pray to God for us, alleluia.*

LEADER:

*Rejoice and be glad, O Virgin Mary, alleluia.*

ALL:

*For the Lord has truly risen, alleluia.*

LEADER:

*Let us pray.*

*God of life,*
*you have given joy to the world*
*by the resurrection of your Son, our Lord*
    *Jesus Christ.*
*Through the prayers of his mother, the Virgin Mary,*
*bring us to the happiness of eternal life.*
*We ask this through Christ our Lord.*

ALL:

*Amen.*[26]

# The Memorare

The author of this intercessory prayer to Mary is unknown, though it is traditionally ascribed to St. Bernard of Clairvaux. It has been widely used for at least five hundred years.

*Remember, most loving Virgin Mary,*
*never was it heard*
*that anyone who turned to you for help*
*was left unaided.*

*Inspired by this confidence,*
*though burdened by my sins,*
*I run to your protection*
*for you are my mother.*

*Mother of the Word of God,*
*do not despise my words of pleading*
*but be merciful and hear my prayer.*
*Amen.*[27]

. . . and she conceived of the Holy Spirit.

# The Angelus

This is traditionally prayed three times a day: in the early morning, at noon, and at the end of the workday. Bells of many Catholic churches still sound the Angelus as a reminder of the presence of Christ in our daily lives.

LEADER:

*The angel spoke God's message to Mary,*

ALL:

*and she conceived of the Holy Spirit.*

*Hail, Mary.*

LEADER:

*"I am the lowly servant of the Lord:*

ALL:

*let it be done to me according to your word."*

*Hail, Mary.*

LEADER:

*And the Word became flesh*

ALL:

*and lived among us.*

*Hail, Mary.*

LEADER:

*Pray for us, holy Mother of God,*

ALL:

*that we may become worthy of the promises of Christ.*

*Let us pray.*

*Lord,*

*fill our hearts with your grace:*

*once, through the message of an angel*

*you revealed to us the incarnation of your Son;*

*now, through his suffering and death*

*lead us to the glory of his resurrection.*

*We ask this through Christ our Lord.*

ALL:

*Amen.*[28]

# Hail, Holy Queen

In Latin this prayer is known as Salve Regina. The text was probably composed in the eleventh century by Hermann the Lame, a monk of Reichenau. It was frequently said as part of the Divine Office, the church's daily prayer.

*Hail, holy Queen, Mother of mercy,*
*hail, our life, our sweetness, and our hope.*
*To you we cry, the children of Eve;*
*to you we send up our sighs,*
*mourning and weeping in this land of exile.*
*Turn, then, most gracious advocate,*
*your eyes of mercy toward us;*
*lead us home at last*
*and show us the blessed fruit of your womb, Jesus:*
*O clement, O loving, O sweet Virgin Mary.*[25]

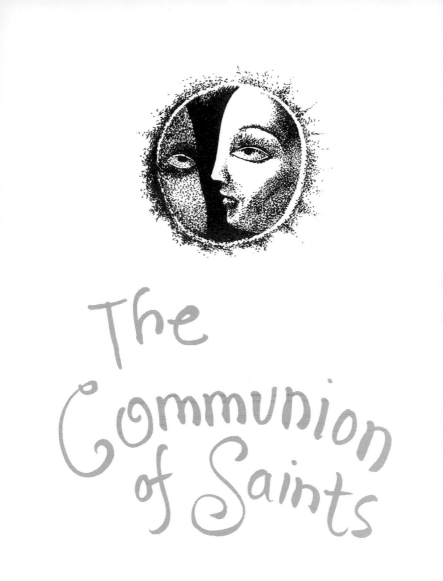

The Communion
of Saints

chapter eight

The Catholic church honors holy men and women, called saints, who are models for us of the Christian life. While we worship God alone, we honor and venerate the saints. In prayer, we ask the saints to intercede for us before God, just as we might ask a friend or family member to pray for us when we have special needs. Scripture commands us to pray for one another (see, for example, James 5:13–18), and God often blesses us in response to prayers from our friends the saints.

Here are some favorite prayers to saints and by saints, as well as one on behalf of our deceased loved ones, who are also part of "the communion of saints."

# A Prayer to St. Joseph

St. Joseph, Mary's husband, is the patron saint of the universal church, of workers, of fathers, and of the dying (among other things). Little is known about him beyond what is found in the Gospel accounts, primarily that he was a carpenter and of the house of David. St. Joseph's feast day is celebrated on March 19, and the Feast of St. Joseph the Worker is celebrated on May 1.

*Most faithful guardian of Jesus and spouse of Mary,*
*you know the anguish of my heart and the*
    *complexity of my problem.*
*Obtain for me the light of the Holy Spirit*
*and all the help I need to enable me at all times and*
    *in all things*
*to fulfill the will of God.*

*I choose you this day, in the presence of Jesus*
  *and Mary,*
*as my counsel, to direct me in all necessities.*
*Guide me as I trust in God to strengthen my heart*
  *during my earthly pilgrimage.*

*Amen.*

# St. Patrick's Breastplate

St. Patrick was a bishop and apostle to Ireland in the fifth century, and he is that country's patron saint today. Legends about him include his use of the shamrock to teach the concept of the Trinity and his driving of snakes from Ireland. His feast day is celebrated March 17.

*Christ, be with me, Christ before me, Christ*
*    behind me,*
*Christ in me, Christ beneath me, Christ above me,*
*Christ on my right, Christ on my left,*
*Christ where I live, Christ where I sit, Christ where*
*    I arise,*
*Christ in the heart of every person who thinks of me,*
*Christ in the mouth of every person who thinks*
*    of me,*

*Christ in the mouth of every person who speaks*
   *of me,*
*Christ in every eye that sees me,*
*Christ in every ear that hears me.*

*Salvation is of the Lord.*
*Salvation is of the Lord,*
*Salvation is of the Christ.*

*May your salvation, O Lord, be ever with us.*

# Make Me an Instrument of Your Peace

St. Francis was born in the twelfth century in Assisi, Italy, and is the founder of the religious community that bears his name, the Franciscans. He is remembered for living simply, caring for the poor, creating the Christmas custom of Nativity scenes, repairing churches, and caring for animals. He is a patron saint of Italy (with St. Catherine of Siena) and of the environment. His feast day is celebrated October 4. This prayer is often attributed to him.

*Lord, make me an instrument of your peace:*

*where there is hatred, let me sow love;*
*where there is injury, pardon;*
*where there is doubt, faith;*
*where there is despair, hope;*
*where there is darkness, light;*
*and where there is sadness, joy.*

*O Divine Master, grant that I may not so much seek*
*to be consoled, as to console;*
*to be understood, as to understand;*
*to be loved, as to love.*

*For it is in giving that we receive,*
*it is in pardoning that we are pardoned,*
*and it is in dying that we are born to eternal life.*

# A Prayer of St. Catherine of Siena

Catherine of Siena is known as a "Doctor of the Church." This fourteenth-century Dominican nun advised popes and wrote several great spiritual works. She is patron saint of nursing and of Italy (with St. Francis of Assisi). Her feast day is April 29.

*You, O God, are a fire that takes away the coldness,*
*illuminates the mind with its light,*
*and causes me to know your truth.*
*And I know that you are beauty and wisdom itself.*
*The food of the angels, you give yourself to us in the*
*fire of your love.*

You,
O God,
are a fire
that takes away
the coldness.

# A Prayer of St. Ignatius of Loyola

In the sixteenth century St. Ignatius of Loyola founded the religious community known as the Society of Jesus, or Jesuits. His manual for spiritual growth, *Spiritual Exercises,* is still widely used today. He is the patron saint of spiritual exercises and retreats; his feast day is July 31.

*Lord Jesus Christ,*
*take all my freedom,*
*my memory, my understanding, and my will.*
*All that I have and cherish*
*you have given me.*

*I surrender it all to be guided by your will.*
*Your grace and your love*
*are wealth enough for me.*
*Give me these, Lord Jesus,*
*and I ask for nothing more.*[29]

# A Prayer of St. Thérèse of Lisieux

Also known as the "Little Flower" and Thérèse of the Child Jesus, St. Thérèse of Lisieux was born in France in 1873. At fifteen, she became a Carmelite nun, dying of tuberculosis at the age of twenty-four. In her teaching, Thérèse focuses on how the ordinary events of life can be made extraordinary and holy. She is the patron saint of foreign missions and of Russia; her feast day is October 1.

*After earth's exile, I hope to go and enjoy you in the homeland,*
*but I do not want to lay up merits for heaven.*
*I want to work only for your love.*
*In the evening of this life,*

*I shall appear before you with empty hands,*

*for I do not ask you, Lord, to count my works.*

*All our justice is blemished in your eyes.*

*I wish, then, to be clothed in your own justice*

*and to receive from your love the eternal possession*

*    of yourself.*[30]

# A Prayer of Blessed Elizabeth of the Trinity

Elizabeth (1880–1906) was a French Carmelite nun whose spirituality focused on both the Trinity and Christ. She has been beatified, the second step toward canonization as a saint. Her feast day is November 8.

*O my God, Trinity whom I adore,*

*help me forget myself entirely*

*so as to root myself in you,*

*permanent and peaceful as if my soul were already*
*in eternity.*

*May nothing trouble my peace*

*or make me leave you, O my unchanging God,*

*but may each moment bring me more deeply into*
*your mystery!*

*Grant my soul peace.*

*Make it your heaven,*

*your beloved dwelling and your place of rest.*

*May I never abandon you, but ever dwell there,*

*whole and entire,*

*totally faithful,*

*entirely adoring,*

*and wholly given over to your work of creation.*

# A Prayer for the Dead

"Lord, for your faithful people life is changed, not ended. When the body of our earthly dwelling lies in death we gain an everlasting dwelling place in heaven."[31] This is the substance of Christian belief about death. Because life is changed, not ended, we continue to have communion with all those who have gone before us in death. Our prayers for those who have died, and their prayers for us, are the way we celebrate this relationship.

The Catholic church teaches that there are three states in which souls die, and three corresponding relations with God after death. "Those who die in God's grace and friendship and are perfectly purified live for ever with Christ." These souls remain with God for ever in heaven.

"To die in mortal sin without repenting and accepting God's merciful love means remaining separated from him for ever by our own free choice. This state of definitive self-exclusion from communion with God and the blessed is called 'hell.'" Finally, "all who die in God's grace and friendship, but still imperfectly purified, are indeed assured of their eternal salvation; but after death they undergo purification, so as to achieve the holiness necessary to enter the joy of heaven."[32] This final purification is named purgatory.

When we pray for the dead, we are praying for the souls of those in purgatory, that they may soon be with God in heaven.

*Eternal rest grant to him [her], O Lord,*

*and let perpetual light shine upon him [her];*

*May his [her] soul and the souls of all the faithful*

  *departed,*

*through the mercy of God,*

*rest in peace.*

*Amen.*

# Prayers of Praise

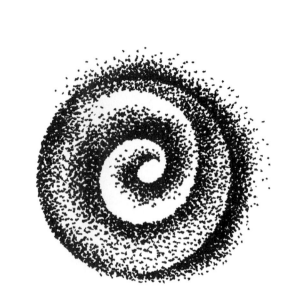

## chapter nine

At certain times, almost everybody prays. We pray when we're frightened or lonely, when we need something desperately, or when we want it very much. We pray when something big is happening in our lives—a new baby, a marriage, a death. And we pray when we are supremely happy.

Happy people often sing, and Christians do a lot of singing at church. *Eucharist,* after all, means "gratitude," and a psalm is a kind of song. Here are some model prayers of joy, praise, and thanksgiving.

# A Thank-You Prayer

This short thank-you prayer can be said anytime, anywhere. In church, we say it like this:

*Thanks be to God.*

In everyday language, we might just say:

*Thank you, Jesus.*

Thank you,
Jesus.

# Praise in Heaven

The Book of Revelation includes beautiful prayers of praise. In chapter 7, there is a picture of the church in heaven—people and angels and mysterious creatures all singing praises to God, giving thanks that "the Lamb at the center of the throne will be their shepherd, and he will guide them to springs of the water of life, and God will wipe away every tear from their eyes." This is their song:

*Salvation belongs to our God*
*who is seated on the throne, and to the Lamb!*

*Amen! Blessing and glory and wisdom*
*and thanksgiving and honor*
*and power and might*
*be to our God forever and ever!*

*Amen.*

REVELATION 7:10, 12

# Praise the Lord!

In this happy song, the whole world is praising God. Read it in unison or antiphonally, alternating lines. Let the children add names of other creatures that praise God!

*Praise the Lord!*

*Praise the Lord from the heavens; praise him in the heights!*
*Praise him, all his angels; praise him, all his host!*
*Praise him, sun and moon; praise him, all you shining stars!*
*Praise him, you highest heavens, and you waters above the heavens!*

Add other praises from the heavens.

*Praise the Lord from the earth, you sea monsters and*
*all deeps,*
*fire and hail; snow and front, stormy wind fulfilling*
*his command!*
*Mountains and all hills, fruit trees and all cedars!*
*Wild animals and all cattle,*
*creeping things and flying birds!*

Add other praises from created things on earth.

*Kings of the earth and all peoples, princes and all*
*rulers of the earth!*
*Young men and women alike, old and young*
*together!*

Add other praises from human beings.

*Let them praise the name of the Lord,*

*for his name alone is exalted;*

*his glory is above earth and heaven.*

*Praise the Lord!*

FROM PSALM 148

# Praise the Lord!

# Notes

The scripture quotations contained herein are from the New Revised Standard Version Bible: Catholic Edition copyright © 1993 and 1989 by the Division of Christian Education of the National Council of the Churches of Christ in the U.S.A. Used by permission. All rights reserved.

Excerpts from *Book of Blessings: Additional Blessings for Use in the United States* © 1988 United States Catholic Conference, Inc., Washington, DC. Used with permission. All rights reserved.

Excerpts from the English translation of *Catechism of the Catholic Church* for use in the United States of America © 1993, United States Catholic Conference, Inc.—Libreria Editrice Vaticana. Used with permission.

English translation of the *Gloria,* Nicene Creed, Apostles' Creed, Sanctus, Doxology, Canticle of Zechariah, and Canticle of Mary by the International Consultation on English Texts.

Excerpts from the English translation of *The Roman Missal* © 1973, International Committee on English in the Liturgy, Inc. (ICEL); excerpts from the English translation of *The Liturgy of the Hours* © 1974, ICEL; excerpts from the English translation of *Rite of Penance* © 1974, ICEL; excerpts from the English translation of *A Book of Prayers* © 1982, ICEL; excerpts from the English translation of *Book of Blessings* © 1988, ICEL. All rights reserved.

[1] *Catechism of the Catholic Church* (Chicago: Loyola University Press, 1994), 2763.

[2] *A Book of Prayers* (1982).

[3] *A Book of Prayers*.

[4] *Book of Blessings* (Collegeville, Minnesota: The Liturgical Press, 1989), *190, 192*.

[5] *Book of Blessings, 194*.

[6] Both birthday blessings are from *Book of Blessings, 336*.

[7] *Book of Blessings, 402*.

[8] The prayers in this chapter are from *The Roman Missal* (New York: Catholic Book Publishing Co., 1973).

[9] *Shorter Christian Prayer* (New York: Catholic Book Publishing Co., 1988), *30*.

[10] *Shorter Christian Prayer, 43*.

[11] *Shorter Christian Prayer, 44*.

[12] This version of Luke 1:68–79 is from *The Liturgy of the Hours* (1974), *13*.

[13] *Shorter Christian Prayer, 30*.

[14] *Shorter Christian Prayer, 30*.

[15] *Shorter Christian Prayer, 37*.

[16] *Shorter Christian Prayer, 38*.

[17] This version of Luke 1:46–55 is from *The Liturgy of the Hours*.

[18] *Shorter Christian Prayer, 34*.

[19] *Book of Blessings, 1537–1540*.

[20] The weekly Advent prayers are adapted from *The Roman Missal*.

[21] *Book of Blessings, 1569*.

[22] *Book of Blessings, 1592, 1595–6*.

[23] *Rite of Penance* (Washington, DC: United States Catholic Conference, 1974), *45*.

[24] *Book of Blessings, 1723*.

[25] *A Book of Prayers, 24*.

[26] *A Book of Prayers, 30*.

[27] *A Book of Prayers, 25.*

[28] *The Roman Missal, 29.*

[29] *A Book of Prayers, 10.*

[30] Adapted from "Act of Offering" in *Story of a Soul,* tr. John Clarke (Washington, DC: ICS, 1981), 277.

[31] Excerpt from Preface for Masses for the Dead from *The Roman Missal.*

[32] *Catechism of the Catholic Church, 1023, 1033, 1030.*

# Index of First Words

# Index of Prayers

# Index of Prayers and
# Readings from Scripture